PRESENTED BY

ℳerritt Stembler '86

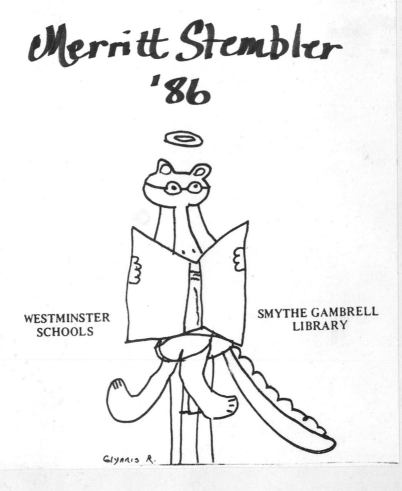

WESTMINSTER
SCHOOLS

SMYTHE GAMBRELL
LIBRARY

Glynnis R.

GOING TO
SCHOOL
IN 1876

The Modern Country Schoolhouse

John J. Loeper

GOING TO SCHOOL IN 1876

ILLUSTRATED WITH OLD PRINTS

Atheneum 1984 *New York*

LIBRARY OF CONGRESS CATALOGING IN PUBLICATION DATA

Loeper, John J.
Going to school in 1876.

SUMMARY: Describes the life of school children in
1876—their dress, teachers, schoolhouses, books,
lessons, discipline, and pastimes, Sequel to "Going
to School in 1776."
1. Education—United States—History—Juvenile
literature. 2. Schools—United States—History—
Juvenile literature. [1. Schools—History. 2. United
States—Social life and customs—1865–1918] I. Title.
LA216.L63 1984   370'.973   83-15669
ISBN 0-689-31015-3

Published simultaneously in Canada by
McClelland & Stewart, Ltd.
Composition by Maryland Linotype, Baltimore, Maryland
Printed and bound by Fairfield Graphics,
Fairfield, Pennsylvania
Designed by Mary Ahern
First Edition

To Jane

Contents

GOING TO
SCHOOL
IN 1876

America in 1876

It was like a birthday party, the Fourth of July and a family celebration all wrapped up into one. And, it lasted all year! It was 1876, the one hundredth birthday of the United States of America. A giant exhibition marked the occasion. Held in Philadelphia, it opened on May 10, 1876. President Ulysses S. Grant was there as well as dignitaries from all over the globe.

The thirteen original states had grown into thirty-seven. The population had increased to 46 million people. That number was growing daily as immigrants arrived to share in the American dream. The worst wounds of the Civil War had healed, and the western wilderness had given way to farms and settlements. Railroads linked the country from coast to coast, and new inventions promised to simplify living. Americans looked back with pride on one hundred years of progress.

Before the Centennial Exhibition closed before New Year's Day of 1877, one out of every fifteen Americans had come to see it. They examined countless displays. There were exhibits sent by foreign countries. There were displays set up by American industry. The women were intrigued by an array of sewing machines. Children admired toys and drank soda from "soda fountains." Men were awed by huge steam engines and locomotives. Everyone marvelled at Alexander Graham Bell's invention, the telephone. If America had accomplished this much in one hundred years, the next one hundred years would be even better.

"We are a perfect nation," one politician boasted in a Centennial speech. But the country was far from perfect. America faced problems with labor, civil rights, immigration, Indian wars and poverty.

America was still a rural society. Most Americans lived on farms or in small villages. There were less than a dozen large cities. Effective mass communication had not yet arrived. Newspapers had limited circulation, and some villages depended on traveling peddlers to bring them news of the outside world.

Some of the news in 1876 was disturbing. In June, the country learned of the massacre of General George Custer and his troops at the Battle of Little Big Horn. November brought news of a disputed presidential election. Both candidates, Rutherford B. Hayes and Samuel J. Tilden, claimed victory at the polls. Eventually, an electoral commission gave the presidency to Hayes. In other news, the nation heard about the publication of Mark Twain's newest book, *The Adventures of Tom Sawyer*.

While the nation celebrated and contemplated its problems, everyday life continued. People were born and died; worked and played; laughed and cried. Men plowed fields and women baked bread and children went to school.

The schools of 1876 were as diverse as the land. Each had its own purpose. There was little uniformity. Not everyone agreed on taxation for education. Many resented "paying for the schooling of rich and poor alike."

First School Building in Cleveland

Gone were the blab schools and dame schools of earlier times. Progress had been made. Teachers were better prepared, and many states had education laws. Yet, not every child went to school. Many worked in mills and mines. Others stayed home.

The American countryside was dotted with schoolhouses. Some were adequate; others were not. There were private schools and public schools; city schools and country schools. Some schools served only certain children; others tried to serve all.

To discover something about being a child and going to school in 1876, we must travel back over the highways of history to other places and other times.

Being a Child in 1876

Ten-year-old Jim Porter hears his mother call.

"Wake up, James! You have chores to do!"

The boy opens his eyes and throws back the covers.

Meanwhile, in back yards roosters cry the coming of day. In stables horses whinny and cows bellow to be milked. Down in the back yard the household cat stalks the hedgerows in search of a morning mouse, and Ginger, the dog, stretchs and yarns. The village of Broxbury, Massachusetts, is awakening to another day.

Before breakfast Jim must carry in wood for the stove and pump the morning supply of water. Then he must milk the family cow. His two sisters are already at work in the kitchen. They help their mother prepare breakfast. Eggs must be gathered from the henhouse and cornmeal sifted and measured.

Broxbury is a typical village of 1876. It has a church, a school, a general store, a law office, an apothecary and a tavern. The village is built around a tree-lined square, with the church at one end and the tavern at the other. The majority of village houses are small and surrounded by picket fences. A few are large. These are owned by merchants and are two or three stories tall. Many communities of the nineteenth century pattern themselves after the New England village plan. Similar villages can be found in the South and Midwest.

Most families in Broxbury have vegetable gardens and fruit trees in their backyards. All have barns or stables to house the family horse and cow. Some families keep pigs, goats and chickens. Every villager—whether merchant, minister or lawyer—is also part farmer. Milk, butter, eggs and vegetables are produced at home. Other provisions come from the general store. Here a customer can buy everything from sugar to furniture.

The chores done and breakfast finished, Jim and his sisters leave the house. At eight o'clock every morning the schoolhouse bell rings calling Broxbury's children to school. Most children of a certain age attend the one-room village school. Massachusetts has had a compulsory attendance law since 1852. It requires school attendance for children between the ages of eight and fourteen for twelve weeks a year. However, the law is never enforced. If a child finds school unpleasant or has a "run-in" with the teacher, he or she just quits and nothing is done about it. Last spring Jim's cousin quit school. Sometimes Jim would like to do the same, but his parents would not approve.

The Broxbury school is a district school. Parents pay a fee or "rate" to a local school committee for each day a child attends school. Tuition amounts to a few cents a day.

The village schoolmaster teaches "reading, writing and ciphering" to all grades.

Life in Broxbury is usually busy. While the men work at farming or business, housewives cook, churn, clean and do the family wash. A few are lucky enough to have "hired girls" to help them. All boys and girls have chores to do before and after school.

Although the people are hard workers, they have their fun. Winter brings skating and sleighing parties. Warm weather brings picnics and swimming in the village pond.

Occasionally some folks visit Boston. Broxbury is a stop on the Boston Railroad Line. Jim went to Boston once with his parents. It was exciting to visit the city and see the big stores and theaters. But he was happy to return to Broxbury. Although it is small, it is a good place to live. He knows everyone in town, and everyone knows him.

In 1876, most Americans live in small towns.

* * *

Life in Coaldale, Pennsylvania is much different for ten-year-old Patrick Doherty. Patrick works as a coal miner. Every day, except Sunday, he and other boys go underground to work in the mines. For their labor, they receive a few pennies a day.

Patrick tells about his work:

> I used to work above ground, but now I go down with the men. I help them by fetching tools and loading the coal into carts. On winter days it is dark when I go down and dark when I come up. There are weeks when I never see the sunlight. It's hard and dirty work. My body is black with coal dust, and my limbs ache. Though I'm still a boy, they expect a man's work from me.

In 1876 there are few child labor laws. Those in force are mild and full of loopholes. One such law is typical: no child of less than fifteen years of age can work more than ten hours a day without the written consent of parent or guardian. Unfortunately, many parents are desperate enough to give their permission. Close to two million children are working full time in 1876. Many work in factories for ten to sixteen hours a day. Others work in the mines or in construction.

Child labor is cheap labor. There are those adults who claim that child labor is a good thing. They say that poor children are better off in a factory or a mine. Furthermore they insist that a child has a constitutional right to work. They accuse those who want to regulate child labor and protect children from exploitation of being "soft" and "silly."

Patrick is one of eight children in the Doherty family. His parents came to Pennsylvania from Ireland. Patrick's father is a miner, and he joined his father in the mines last year. His younger brothers work as "colliery boys." Colliery is another name for coal mine. Colliery boys pick pieces of rock and slate from the mined coal. By day's end many young hands are raw and bleeding.

Patrick's day begins at five o'clock in the morning. By six he is deep in the bowels of the earth. The job is unhealthy and dangerous. There is poor ventilation in the mines and the air is heavy with dust. Frequently there is a "cave-in." Unsupported earth comes tumbling down, often trapping miners for hours or forever. For light, the miners wear small oil lamps on their hats.

Patrick's shift is over at four in the afternoon. He returns home and washes the coal dirt from his body using a tub in the backyard. After supper he goes to bed. He must work again in the morning. There is no time for play or fun. Sunday is his only day of rest.

Sunday morning is spent in church. After service, Patrick and other children attend a Sunday school in the church basement. As there is no school in Coaldale, the church offers some instruction in reading and religion. Because children work, many churches offer a Sunday school. It is the only school these children have.

Patrick's town, Coaldale, was built in 1850 by the Pennsylvania Coal Company. It is a company town. All the buildings including the general store are owned by the

A Woman and a Boy Weighing Coal

company. Miners not only work for the company but pay the company rent for their homes. The company built the church, but refuses to build a school.

"There is no need for a school," a company official insists. "Our children learn all they need to know in the mines!"

It will be many years before children like Patrick have schools.

* * *

Twelve-year-old Jim Wright was born in Maryland but now lives in Iowa. In 1870, his father was taken by a case of "western fever." Iowa seemed a land of promise, so the Wright family packed its household goods in wagons and went west. Jim's father bought some farmland there and built a cabin for his family. The cabin is near a small lake. This provides a supply of fish and a summer "swimmin' hole." The surrounding woods have an abundance of game: deer, pheasants, quail, squirrels and rabbits. Foxes and coyotes are numerous. Occasionally a herd of buffalo or elk pass by.

The farm grows wheat, oats and barley. Livestock consists of chickens, ducks, cows and pigs.

Jim's day begins at 5 A.M. with breakfast. Then there are chores: milk the cows, slop the pigs, care for the chickens and work the fields. At harvest, Jim must thrash the grain. Sheaves of grain are spread on the barn floor. Then, astride a horse, Jim goes round and round thrashing out the grain underfoot.

Recess

During the winter months, Jim and his younger sister go to school. The schoolhouse is a small log building, eighteen by twenty-four feet. At each end of the room is a small window with eight panes of glass. In the center of the room is the teacher's desk and a large iron stove. Benches for the students are arranged around three sides of the room. These have no backs and are easily tipped over. Often, a bench of squirming children falls to the floor.

Parents decide how long children should attend school. Mr. Wright thinks that a few weeks each winter is quite enough. There are times, especially during the planting and harvesting seasons, when work is more important than school.

Free tax-supported schools were instituted in Iowa in 1834, when the land was part of the Michigan Territory. After Iowa became a state in 1846, a system of public schools was established. However, attendance is not compulsory.

Farm children are expected to work. Farming is a family affair. Every member of the household is expected to contribute. Jim's sister helps with housework, and Jim helps to tend the fields and animals. A verse in Jim's reading book tells the story:

> *Though little, I work*
> *As hard as a Turk,*
> *When you give me employ.*
> *I can plow and sow*
> *And reap and mow,*
> *I am a farmer's boy.*

* * *

At least families in rural America have fresh air and sunshine. Many families in 1876 do not. They live in crowded city slums.

For children sleeping here, their lullabies are street sounds. Their playgrounds are alleyways. Their fun is whatever can be found amid poverty and want.

Growing numbers of immigrants coming to American cities have to be accommodated. Rather than spread out, cities decide to build up. Tenements are erected. The tenement is a tall building containing apartments for many families. In fast-growing cities builders crowd tenements together and pay little attention to living space and facilities. One outside water tap and one outdoor toilet might serve an entire building. Water for cooking and washing is hauled in buckets. Baths are taken in wooden washtubs.

Conditions in the tenements are terrible. Many people are crowded into a few rooms. In one Chicago tenement sixteen people live in one room. Dirt and garbage collect in narrow, stuffy hallways and breed disease. There is always the danger of fire.

Eight-year-old Tony Wasic lives in such a building on the lower East side in New York City. The Wasic family emigrated from Poland. Political and religious persecution there forced them to leave. The New World offered a new beginning. The Wasics share a tenement with eighty other families. Their quarters consist of two rooms. Mother, father, Tony and his two younger brothers live there.

During the day, Tony attends a city school. Since 1867, the state of New York has provided free, public schools for all of its children. The immigrant children are taught English, American history and civics. The school is expected to be a "melting pot" where children from different lands are taught to be Americans. Tony and his brothers have learned to speak English. Their parents find the language difficult to learn, so at home Polish is spoken.

After school, Tony works as a newsboy. He stands on a street corner selling newspapers in all kinds of weather. In rain, snow or bitter cold, he must stand until his papers are sold. For this he earns a penny a day. Many children work after school to earn extra money for their families. They sell flowers or matches in the streets. Others are newsboys or shoeshine boys. Some simply beg pennies from strangers. In 1876 over eighty percent of American families earn less than four hundred dollars a year. Immi-

Newsboys Waiting for Papers

grant families have a hard time. "Greenhorns," as immigrants are called, take any job they can find.

Someday Tony hopes to own a grocery store. His father tells him that in America anything is possible. He pictures himself in a white apron standing behind a counter selling fruits and vegetables. If he works hard, his dream may come true.

Many brave men and women live in the tenements of America. They keep their pride and look forward to better days. But the discouragements are many. It is hard to keep faith while living in poverty.

* * *

"Once we were a proud people," Anna Crowfoot's mother tells her. "We owned our land, and our people honored the ancient traditions."

Twelve-year-old Anna Crowfoot lives in Indian Territory. She is a member of the Cherokee tribe.

In 1876 the eastern half of Oklahoma is called Indian Territory. It is populated by Choctaws, Cherokees, Creeks, Chickasaws and Seminoles. In 1830, the Indians in various places were ordered to leave their ancestral homes and move to this territory. This was done to gain control of rich tribal lands. The Indians, especially the Cherokees, resisted. But government troops were used to force them into the territory.

Anna attends the Cherokee Female Seminary. Both male and female schools have existed in the territory since 1851. These schools give instruction in farming and the domestic arts. Anna learns sewing, cooking and the preparation of herbal medicines. Boys learn how to plant and farm.

Few people in 1876 take the education of Indian children seriously. Those who do are convinced that education will "civilize" the Indians and win them away from "savage ways." Some want to convert them to Christianity. Few people are interested in Indian history or tribal culture. Indian children must learn these at home. Anna often sits by her mother's side listening to tales of the Cherokee tribe and their great leader, Sequoyah. It was Sequoyah who invented an alphabet and taught the Indians how to read and write.

Anna enjoys going to school and learning some of the white man's ways. But she also wants to preserve her Indian heritage. She is proud of her people. Someday she hopes to become a teacher and open a Cherokee school. Here children would be taught lessons and tribal customs.

Right now there are few schools for Indians. Although no accurate figures are available, it is estimated that less than fifteen hundred Indian children attend school in 1876.

* * *

In the middle of the lace-covered table in the spacious dining room is a birthday cake. It is covered with white icing and decorated with pink candy rosebuds. Surrounding the cake are crystal bowls of freshly made ice cream and sugared strawberries. Everything is ready for Nancy Feather's eleventh birthday.

Nancy is fortunate. Her father owns a hardware store in Oakdale, Indiana. Like many other Americans, he and his family live a comfortable life. Their homes are neat and roomy. Their gardens are neatly trimmed. Their rooms are decorated with rugs and elegant furniture.

In Oakdale, Mr. Feather is a respected man. He is a good provider and takes pride in his country and his community. He is a member of the so-called "middle class"— professional and business people.

Those to whom success is given live a good life. In an age of low prices and light taxation, there is money to spend on luxuries. Every August the Feather family moves to a summer house at Elk Lake. They have a cook and a gardener and own a coach and four.

Most members of the middle class are serious about social approval. They feel that they must set an example to others. Children are scrubbed and sent off to church on Sunday morning in starched shirts and dresses. Etiquette is

important. "Little born ladies and gentlemen should not keep uncultivated company" one etiquette book warns parents. Education and culture are prized. Most homes boast a piano or a library.

Entering the dining room, Nancy is greeted by a chorus of "Happy Birthday." Then the cake is cut and the festivities begin. Her aunts and uncles and little cousins are all guests at the party. Each has brought a present. One gives Nancy a book of poetry. Another brings a music box. An uncle gives her a five dollar gold piece.

In the morning, Nancy will bring the music box to school to share with her classmates. She attends Miss Dwight's Academy. The Academy teaches "Young people of quality music, art, elocution, classical literature and French conversation."

The gap between the advantaged and the disadvantaged is very obvious in 1876.

How Children Dress in 1876

FRED HART'S WOOLEN SUIT.

ANNA JENKINS'S FLOUR SACK.

WILLIAM SMITH GOES TO CHURCH.

LUCY PRESTON VISITS HER GRANDMOTHER.

MARY TRENT'S LETTER TO HER COUSIN.

On the Fourth of July, 1876, nine-year-old Fred Hart examines his new suit. He will wear it to watch the Centennial parade in his hometown.

Fred's mother made the suit from a bolt of gray woolen cloth. It has a pair of long trousers and a form-fitting, waist-length jacket. Under the jacket, Fred will wear a long-sleeved cotton shirt with a black string tie.

Fred feels the material. It is coarse and scratchy.

"Do I have to wear it?" he asks his mother. "It's too hot!"

"Of course you have to wear it!" she scolds. "I don't want you to catch a chill."

Many mothers worry about their children's health. There are, of course, no immunizing shots to prevent disease. Mothers have their own ideas on how to prevent illness. One stand-by is heavy clothing in all kinds of weather. It prevents sudden "chills."

Much of the blame for the discomfort of woolen clothing in warm weather lies at the door of a German doctor, Gustav Jaeger. Dr. Jaeger claims that to wear a vegetable fiber, like cotton or linen, is practically poisonous. They do not absorb the body's "exhalations." Wool does. He teaches that good health requires wool in contact with the body. He also believes it must be tight-fitting

to allow the least possible movement of air along the skin.

Although Fred is not anxious to wear his woolen suit on a hot day, he would rather not catch a "chill." Fighting a cold in 1876 means large doses of castor oil and camphor grease rubbed on chest and feet. A foul-tasting and smelly cure!

Not everyone concurred with Dr. Jaeger's point of view. One writer of the period pleaded:

> What children need is perfect freedom—
> freedom to romp, to make mudpies, to leap
> fences, to fish, to climb trees, to chase butterflies,
> to gather wildflowers, to do all those things that
> healthy childhood delights in and to do them in
> comfortable clothing designed for that purpose.

Fred would agree.

* * *

Unlike Fred, there are other children who have little to wear.

In a New England mill town, little Anna Jenkins catches her reflection in a shop window. She is not as prettily dressed as other children passing by. Her dress is a flour sack with holes cut in it for her head and arms. Over her shoulders she wears a tattered woolen shawl—her only protection against the weather. Anna's family is too poor to buy regular clothing. They must make do with what they have. Her father works in a mill, and his meager salary hardly pays for food and shelter.

Anna dreams of owning a pretty dress someday. It will be made of white silk and be covered with laces and ribbons.

As she looks at her reflection, she smooths her hair and pulls at her sack dress. She imagines that she is wearing the white gown.

"My, what a beautiful dress!" people admire.

"Thank you," Anna replies. "I have so many pretty dresses it is difficult to decide which one to wear."

"Get away from here!" A harsh voice interrupts her reverie. It is the shopkeeper. He has seen her in front of his shop and is annoyed.

"Little urchin!" he shouts. "Go back to the slums where you belong!"

* * *

"William! Hurry up! Church service begins at eleven!"

Upstairs, ten-year-old William Smith combs his hair. He wants it to be just right. Carefully, he parts it in the middle, sweeping both sides back over his ears. This is the current style, although some men and boys insist on parting their hair to one side.

Satisfied, he looks in a mirror to admire himself. He looks quite handsome in his sailor suit. This is a very popular fashion worn by boys. The bell bottom pants and navy blouse are made of blue serge, a woolen fabric. The suit has a wide nautical collar edged in red and white cord.

And, around his neck, suspended on a thin chain, is a wooden whistle. No sailor suit is complete without a whistle!

"William! Hurry up! Your father is waiting for you in the horse and buggy!"

"Coming, Mother," William answers. He smooths his hair with his hands, then hurries down the stairs. As he runs along, he toots on his whistle.

"Stop that noise, William," his mother orders. "Good boys do not make noise on Sundays!"

There are times when William would rather not be a good boy. But, for now, he has no choice.

* * *

Every Saturday afternoon, young Lucy Preston visits her grandmother. Her grandmother lives in a big house on the other side of town. Lucy enjoys going there for tea and cake. She spends what her grandmother calls, "a sociable afternoon."

Lucy's grandmother believes that, "a young lady should wear a proper costume, fashionable and pretty, and behave in a proper manner."

For today's visit, Lucy will wear a pink dress with a full skirt caught up at the sides with rosettes. This will show off the several petticoats of crinoline underneath. A sash of blue ribbon tied at the back will reach to the hem of her skirt. This is below the knees. Unlike the grown ladies of this period, her dress will not be full length. She will wear a ribboned bonnet and white kid gloves. Long stockings and high, buttoned shoes will complete her costume.

A poem in a lady's magazine reminds fashionable girls that:

> *We are fond of little bonnets,*
> *Of skirts quite full and wide,*
> *And we want our pretty petticoats*
> *To show off at our sides.*

For the most part, children's dress is an imitation of adult fashion. One child of the period complains in her diary, "How my gown, petticoats, crinolines, ribbons, ties, cloaks, hats, bonnets, gloves, capes, hooks, buttons and all the other items of a girl's costume annoy and irritate me."

But, as Lucy Preston's grandmother is fond of saying: Style requires sacrifice.

* * *

In March of 1876, twelve-year-old Mary Trent writes to her young cousin:

Dearest Jane,
I must tell you my news! Today I became a
stylish young lady. Mother bought me a corset to
keep my waist pulled in. I tried it on and can
hardly breathe while wearing it. Yet, it is
necessary if I am to wear my new gown. It has a
tight waist and bodice, and the skirt has over
twenty yards of silk fabric. Most exciting of all,
it has a bustle! A framework of coiled wire and
pads of cotton keep the cloth elegantly draped
behind me. And as I walk along, the skirt sweeps
the floor. It is fashioned after a Paris creation.
Mother also bought me a new pair of kid shoes.
They wrap my ankles and each shoe has fifteen
buttons. They are difficult to put on, but I do
think it is important to be properly dressed,
don't you agree?
Next month I am going to Chicago. Aunt Martha
has inivited me to stay with her. I plan to bring
my walking dress, my morning dress, a riding
outfit, a church dress and, of course, my new silk
dress. I shall need all of them.
Father became angry with me yesterday. He said
that I am far too interested in buttons, bows,
ribbons and laces. Poor dear! He just does not
understand. All that a man needs is a suit for
work and another for church. We proper ladies

must have an outfit for every occasion.
Do write and tell me about your wardrobe. I am
most anxious to hear from you.

As ever,
your cousin, Mary

The Schools of 1876

The Wexbury District School in Wexbury, Connecticut, is located on the old Post Road. It is about one mile outside of town. All students, regardless of distance, walk to school. The school is a small, one-room, wooden building. It has a low bell tower at one end of a shingled roof. It is painted gray and looks quite dingy. Behind the schoolhouse are two outhouses for the "retirement of either sex."

In 1876, most public schools are known as district schools. This means that a particular school serves a designated area.

The Wexbury District School, like most others, is controlled by a school committee. In Pennsylvania, these officials are called school directors. In other states the committee is called a school board.

The school committee maintains the building and pays the teacher through taxation. However, costs are low. Custodial work is done by teachers, who earn very little—perhaps four to twelve dollars a month.

In Wexbury there is one teacher for all grades. Some district schools in larger towns or cities have buildings with more than one room and several teachers.

Completion of the elementary program at the district school ends the formal education of most students. There are few public high schools. And, with weak attendance laws, truancy is high. The Wexbury school reports that more than half its "scholars" are absent on an average day.

Inside the Wexbury school are five rows of double wooden desks with attached seats. These are fastened to the floor with screws. At one end of the room there is a high desk on a raised platform for the teacher. The school boasts new-fangled "blackboard." Many folks in 1876 consider these to be a passing fancy. It also has one world globe, one map of the United States, one unabridged dictionary and a collection of rocks.

Heat for the school is provided by an iron wood-burning stove. Light for dark days is given by a hanging oil lamp. Drinking water comes from a pail and dipper.

A Connecticut official said recently that "many of our schools are less comfortable than our prisons." There are days when the "scholars" at the Wexbury District School might agree!

* * *

In southern and western states, the district schools often take the name of the community or area. Many of these names are very colorful, like Broken Bone, Sleepy Cat, Cinderella, Disappointment Creek, Dingy Bottom and Bald Knob.

One such school, the Fly Hollow School in West Virginia, serves the rural community of Fly Hollow. Most people in the Hollow are farmers, and the community covers a wide area. Houses and farms are scattered and often far apart.

The Fly Hollow School is a new schoolhouse. In 1872, a new state constitution provided for a system of free public schools in West Virginia, supported by state funds. As a result of this legislation, the Fly Hollow School was constructed in 1874. It is a one-room structure, painted white with green trim.

The school has ten students and one teacher. Like New England schools, it is governed by a school committee.

In rural communities of the period, many residents are related. This is true of Fly Hollow. Simeon Lilly and Cyrus Lilly are members of the school committee. Their cousin, Miss Daisie Lilly, is the teacher. Five of her students are cousins. Two other students are nephews.

Miss Lilly arrives at school each morning at seven. She comes by horse and carriage. Her students arrive at eight. They must walk to school in all kinds of weather. The school is seldom closed.

The Fly Hollow School has three grades—primary, intermediate and upper. A student is passed on to the next grade whenever Miss Lilly feels he or she is ready. Her cousin, Noah Lilly, has been in the primary grade for five years.

"Kinfolk or not," Miss Lilly explains, "he must master his book learnin' before he moves on!"

* * *

A teacher in Colorado complained in 1875, "I am sure there is not another schoolhouse in the nation as primitive as mine!"

But many teachers would not agree, especially Miss Molly Robinson of Logan County, Nebraska. Her schoolhouse, which is also her house, is built of sod!

The pioneer settlers of Nebraska faced many difficulties. Nebraska's climate is unpredictable. There can be extremes of heat and cold. Summers are hot with light rainfall. Winters bring bitter cold and high winds. Vegetation is limited to grasslands and low evergreens. As a result, wood and water, two necessities for living, are scarce.

Many buildings in 1876 are made of sod rather than wood. Oblong pieces are cut out of the surface of the grassland. These sod "bricks" are used for construction. Sod buildings can range from simple cabins to elaborate two-story houses. Miss Robinson's school is a low, single room, sod cabin. It has a dirt floor and a roof made of grass and mud. Each spring, plant roots in the sod cause the schoolhouse to bloom. Tiny prairie wildflowers pop out of the sod bricks and turn the schoolhouse into a spring bouquet. Yet, however colorful the schoolhouse in springtime, it is still a rough, uncomfortable place.

Inside, the teacher has a bed and utensils for cooking as well as a few desks and benches. Miss Robinson lives and works in the same place.

Six pupils attend the sod schoolhouse, and school is conducted every day except Sunday from October to May.

As in other sections of the west, Nebraska's earliest schools were established by missionaries. But after gaining statehood in 1867, Nebraska provided support for free, public education. Miss Robinson's school is supported by state funds.

"I don't mind the place," claims Miss Robinson. "It's not fancy, but we get our work done."

* * *

In September of 1876 the *Millville Gazette* ran the following advertisement:

NOTICE

The Millville Academy

I plan to open a School for Boys on the 26th of October next. The pupils will be taught in my Family Dwelling. Instruction will embrace all branches of Science and Classical Learning. As I will act as teacher with no assistants, the number of students must be limited. There will be two vacations during the year, one in December and one in August. School will be held six days a week. All pupils will be required to study the Bible and to attend worship on the Sabbath. Cost per year, $180.00. Above cost includes Tuition, Books, Fuel and Midday Meal.

Mathias Wilson
SCHOOLMASTER

A growing town is sure to have an academy for the children of local "quality." These are private schools run by ministers or local schoolmasters. The academies stress learning and the social graces. They teach etiquette as well as other subject matter.

Learning to eat properly, speak properly and act properly are an assential part of the curriculum.

Mr. Wilson, the master of the Millville Academy, attended Yale College. He reads both Latin and Greek and is a stern master. Tall, with a red beard, he commands the respect of his boys. At the noonday meal he presides over the dining table. Woe to the boy who spills his soup or forgets to use his napkin! He will be dismissed from the table and locked in a closet.

The regular course at the Academy includes reading, writing, elocution, algebra, geometry and history. For an extra charge of two dollars a week, Mr. Wilson will teach a boy Latin and Greek.

"My boys are prepared to enter the best colleges when they leave my academy," Mr. Wilson boasts.

* * *

If the local "quality" wants literate sons, they also want informed and ladylike daughters. The female seminary is the counterpart of the boys' academy. The typical seminary is taught by some woman of achievement, perhaps one who can speak French or is well read. Often this is a minister's wife or daughter. European women are also in demand. "French and English women of quality exert a noble influence on young ladies attending our school," one advertisement boasts.

A female seminary in Milwaukee, Wisconsin, lists typical subjects offered to young ladies in its annual bulletin:

The Misses Masters' School for Young Ladies
Dobbs-Ferry-on-the-Hudson, N.Y.

The girls will be instructed in spelling, writing, grammar, correspondence, vocal and instrumental music, drawing, embroidery and other fashionable fancy-work.

* * *

On the way to school some young hecklers called out, "Look at that black boy! So uppity he goes to school every day! Must think he's somebody special!" Then they threw rocks at him and made him cry.

Jason attends the Goose Creek School in South Carolina. It is a separate school for black children. Goose Creek is a dingy, two-room cabin. There is one teacher—Miss Bond. She was trained by the American Missionary Society, a philanthropic group interested in the education of black people.

Thirteen other children of all ages go to school with Jason. They learn the basic skills of reading, writing, arithmetic, hygiene and farming.

Before the Civil War, blacks in the south were denied any education. There was no need to educate slaves. However, following the war, southern states passed laws providing for free public education for both blacks and whites. But it is a dual system. They are separate schools for black children and for white children. It is unacceptable at this time for both races to attend the same school. There are even a few who insist that black children need no education and that schools for them are a waste of money.

Some children, both black and white, tease and taunt Jason for wanting to go to school. They call him names, and once someone grabbed and kicked him. But Jason persists. He is determined to learn as much as he can. His mother and teacher help him. They offer support and encouragement.

"You stay in school, Jason, no matter what," his mother tells him.

"I will, Momma," Jason promises.

For many black children of the period, education is a precious gift. It was never possible before.

* * *

For most city children, going to school is commonplace in 1876. Large cities have established school systems.

P.S. 84 is typical of a city school. Unlike its country cousins, it carries a number instead of a name.

The school is located in the heart of the city. It is a two-story brownstone building with four rooms—two up and two down. A wide hallway with a staircase divides the building.

Classrooms are spacious. Children sit in rows of benches facing the teacher and blackboards. The benches are similar to church pews. Class size is large, the average numbering fifty to sixty pupils. School opens at eight in the morning and ends at four in the afternoon.

City schools are administered by a school superintendent, often a political appointment. A frequent criticism made of city schools is that they are politically controlled. Yet they manage to do a good job. They take immigrant children of many nationalities and teach them a new language and a new way of life.

* * *

When Maria first entered St. Luke's Parish School, she was frightened by the nuns. They looked forbidding in their black robes and veils. Now, however, she feels at home with them and enjoys going to school at St. Luke's.

From earliest times America has had church schools. Some of our nation's first schools were established by religious groups. Jews, Protestants and Catholics had educational institutions. There were Quaker schools in Pennsylvania, Lutheran schools in the Midwest, and denominational schools of various sorts in New England. The number of church schools grew, and they are quite common in 1876.

St. Luke's is a Catholic school. It is operated and supported by St. Luke's Catholic parish. It has five levels, with a nun teaching each level. Instruction includes religious training.

Public School Children in New York City
Beginning the Day with Calisthenics

Maria is in the third level. Her teacher is Sister Agnes. Every morning Sister Agnes leads the children in prayer and then instructs them in reading, writing, arithmetic, history and geography. A portion of every afternoon is devoted to studying the catechism. The nuns believe in discipline, and children are expected to study and behave.

There are some Americans who disapprove of church schools.

They claim that they fail to "Americanize" children and expose them to children of all faiths. Yet, in 1876, there are thousands of church schools in the nation.

For Maria, St. Luke's is her school. Although the nuns are strict, she is happy there. Her school and church are an important part of her family life. At night when she says her prayers, she always adds "and bless St. Luke's."

* * *

Five-year-old Jeff cried and cried. He did not want to leave his mother and go to school.

"But you will like kindergarten," his mother coaxed.

"No, I won't!" he bawled.

"You will have toys to play with and be with other boys and girls," his mother continued.

"I don't care," Jeff answered.

Going to kindergarten is a new experience in 1876. There are very few of them. The first public school kindergarten opened in St. Louis only three years before. Since then, other communities are experimenting with the idea.

Kindergarten—a German term for "child's garden"—was the idea of Friedrich Froebel. He was a German educator. To Froebel, the child was a young plant who needed tender care in a special garden. Kindergarten provided a readiness for school.

"Let me have him," the kindergarten teacher suggests as she takes Jeff by the hand. She leads him into a gaily decorated room. When he spies the toys and a big sandbox, he smiles.

"We will have fun here, Jeff," the teachers whispers. "This will be our own special place."

Jeff decides that he may like it, especially the sandbox.

There are some who are opposed to kindergarten. They call it "tomfoolery" and "silliness." One critic claims that the brains of very young children are "not sufficiently developed for instruction."

The Teachers of 1876

AMBROSE HAWKINS PASSES HIS EXAMINATION.

THE TWIN CREEK NORMAL SCHOOL.

FROM *Godey's Lady's Book*.

MISS MOLLY.

AN ITEM FROM THE *Union Daily News*.

"You are Ambrose Hawkins?" asks the County Superintendent of Schools.

"Yes, sir."

"How old are you?"

"I am sixteen, sir."

"You have come to take the teacher examination?"

"Yes, sir."

"First, Hawkins, tell me something about yourself."

"Well, sir, I was born here in Dauphine County and went to the school at White Mountain. After that I worked on a farm to earn my tuition money for high school. I passed the examination and entered Harrisburg High School. There I studied American history, bookkeeping, algebra, surveying and literature."

"Did you take any course related to teaching?"

"No, sir. But I've read Mr. Page's book *The Theory and Practice of Teaching.*"

The superintendent smiles. "There is no other book of such great influence in helping teachers."

At this time in history, the typical rural teacher (and often the city teacher as well) is a person who is either a rural school graduate or a high school graduate. High school graduates are less common. To be appointed to a teaching position requires passing an examination set by a superintendent of schools. Few other qualifications are necessary.

"Are you ready for your examination, Hawkins?" the superintendent asks.

"Yes, sir."

"Then, get your pen ready. I will read the questions."

The examination covers questions in mathematics, history, geography and grammar. Ambrose Hawkins must also write a short essay on the topic, "How the Teacher Benefits Mankind."

The superintendent peers over his glasses. He has read the answers to the questions and the finished essay.

"Congratulations, Hawkins!" he says. "You have passed your examination. In a few weeks I will give you an appointment as teacher in one of the county schools."

* * *

In 1834, two men shared a ship's cabin during a forty-one day passage from Liverpool to New York. One was German, the other American. During the long voyage, the German explained to the American the German method of training teachers. It was a unique idea—people were taught how to teach! The American, Charles Brooks, was enthusiastic about this new idea and decided to promote it in the United States. Through his efforts, normal schools, as they were called, became a part of American education. By 1876, there are over fifty normal schools in the United States. One of these is the Twin Creek Normal School in Minnesota.

At Twin Creek, future teachers study subject matter along with the theory and practice of teaching. Some normal schools even have demonstration classrooms where students can practice teaching.

Twin Creek is a state institution. Other normal schools are county or municipal institutions.

Normal School, Camden, Maine

The students live at Twin Creek. There are both male and female dormitories. It offers a two-year course, but many students do not stay that long. Even with a short stay at the normal school, they find their services as teachers very much in demand. The notion of a trained teacher is very new.

* * *

Godey's Lady's Book is a respected magazine published in Philadelphia. Most American women of this period respect its views.

Women early recognized the attractiveness of teaching. It was one of the few genteel vocations offered to a young woman. Poorly educated girls might become housemaids or factory workers, but a girl with schooling could become a teacher. *Godey's Lady's Book* has always advocated more female teachers in the schools:

Young Women must become the teachers . . . they are the best teachers . . . because of the superior tact and moral power natural to the female character. Women can afford to teach for one-half, or even less, the salary which men would ask, because the female teacher has only to care for herself. She does not look forward to the duty of supporting a family, should she marry. Where female teachers have been hired, they are found faithful and useful.

Eventually, teaching became a woman's profession by default. Officials suddenly realized that a woman was good at teaching. She would work for half the salary a man expected, and her "gentle nature" helped children to learn. Yet, one Michigan official questioned:

Tho' the cheapest guardian and teacher of childhood, can she prepare children for the intellectual demands of the superior male teacher?

* * *

"I love Miss Molly," eight year old Timmy confessed to his brother.

"Don't be stupid!" his brother answered. "Nobody loves the teacher!"

Miss Molly is the teacher at the Center Valley District School. She is nineteen years old and has taught at the school for three years. She is a graduate of a nearby district

school and came to Center Valley after passing her teacher examination. She boards with a local farm family and attends church regularly.

"I don't care!" Timmy protested. "When I grow up, I'm going to marry her."

"Oh, no you're not!" his brother scolded. "Teachers can't get married!"

Should Miss Molly marry, she will have to leave her teaching position. Most school committees disapprove of married female teachers. "You can't run a school and a family at the same time!" one committeeman claims.

Although Miss Molly had no teacher training before coming to Center Valley, she tries to learn about her profession. Twice a year she attends a teacher institute. At the institute teachers from a certain area are brought together for instruction. For several days they are taught subject matter and methods of teaching. Miss Molly also belongs to a teachers' reading circle. At the circle, teachers gather to discuss and share information. Both the reading circle and the institute are meant to train teachers and keep them informed.

At a recent institute, Miss Molly and other teachers learned about the principles of an emerging new subject—psychology. They were most interested as they had never heard of it before.

"Don't you love Miss Molly?" Timmy asked his brother.

"I used to," was the reply. "But, when you are big like me, your lessons get harder and the teacher makes you work. Can't love someone who makes you miserable!"

* * *

The following item is included in a July, 1876, issue of the *Union Daily News:*

Miss Emily Brown of this city has accepted a position to teach all grades in the High Bridge

School. She is well known for her good character and her interest in education. She will live at home with her parents and three brothers and will travel by horse and buggy. The four mile drive to and from her place of employment should prove beneficial to both her health and complexion.

The Lessons of 1876

The children arrive at the country school at eight o'clock in the morning. All walk to school regardless of the weather. Some walk several miles.

Once assembled in the classroom, the day begins with a reading lesson. Although there is a classroom flag, there is no Pledge of Allegiance. This is still twenty years in the future. Nor is there a national anthem to sing. None has been chosen.

"Open your McGuffey Readers, boys and girls," the teacher says. "Today we will read the story of Mary and her lamb and how it followed her to school one day."

Part of America's heritage is being developed by the

reading books in use in 1876. "Mary's Lamb," "Twinkle, Twinkle, Little Star" and "If At First You Don't Succeed, Try, Try Again" became part of our culture through the McGuffey Readers. In schools across the land over one million McGuffey Readers are in use.

The McGuffey Eclectic Readers ("eclectic" means selected from various sources) first appeared around 1836. They contained stories, poems and exercises with a pious or patriotic theme. Millions of American schoolchildren in 1876 read poems about the "Boy on the Burning Deck" and the "Old Oaken Bucket." They read passages from the Bible and Shakespeare. They learn from stories called "Respect for the Sabbath" and "Control Your Temper."

The compiler of the Readers was William Holmes McGuffey. He taught in a country school in Ohio and later became a college professor.

After reading, there is an arithmetic lesson. Mental arithmetic is popular. This is problem solving done without a pencil and paper. Then comes recess.

The children go outside to play and to use the toilets—two wooden sheds or "outhouses." There is one for boys and one for girls.

Recess is followed by a writing lesson using slates. Although paper, pen and pencils are common in 1876, many schools still use slates. A slate is a rectangular piece of good quality slate set in a wooden frame. The pupils write on them with a slate pen, a pointed thin rod of compressed slate powder. Letters and figures can be wiped off readily with a cloth or a shirt sleeve.

At lunchtime the children eat in the classroom. Most bring their lunch, but some will share a pot of soup cooked by the teacher on the classroom stove.

The afternoon is devoted to history and geography. Today the teacher tells the children about Colorado, soon to become the thirty-eighth state in the Union. She explains that next year there will be another star in the flag, representing the newest state. The day ends with a spelling bee, a popular activity in 1876.

Between four and five o'clock in the afternoon, the children leave for home. But the teacher must stay on to clean and sweep the classroom.

* * *

McGuffey selections are called "pieces." Children not only read pieces, but speak them, write them and dramatize them.

The class has decided to dramatize a piece from the Fifth Reader. It offers some good advice.

FIRST READER: I am a stranger here and my horse has fallen through the rotten timbers of the bridge and is drowned. What am I to do? I need him to pull my wagon.

SECOND READER: Look at the poor man. How I pity him.

THIRD READER: I pity him, too.

FOURTH READER: The poor man! What a shame! He has lost his horse.

FIFTH READER: All of you seem to pity this man, but how much? Here, stranger, this is the amount of my pity. Here is a ten dollar bill. If others do as I do, you will be able to get another horse.

FIRST READER: Thank you, sir. A friend in need is a friend, indeed!

* * *

Many children keep copybooks. It is a common practice in schools. In the copybooks pupils record their best work.

Following is a selection from one such copybook. It belongs to ten-year-old Edna Rinker.

My Biography

I will give a sketch of my early years.

I was born near the town of Freemansburg, and there my entire life has been spent so far. My mother says I caused a great deal of trouble when I was young. I suppose this must be the reason I am so quiet at the present time.

When I was about five years old, I attended my first party. All that I can remember of it is that we had ice cream and bananas.

At the age of six years I attended school at Shinersville, where I learned to read, write and spell. There were eight scholars in my class and I remember

the day I went into the First Reader. At recess, we
went onto the playground and amused ourselves with
such games as Tag, Hide and Go Seek and Catch the
Can.

There were two departments in our school, primary
and grammar. When I was eight years old, I was
admitted into the grammar school. About this age,
I used to be very fond of playing with dolls and
making doll clothing. My favorite doll was named
Alice.

At the close of my first year in grammar, we had a
class night. It was a very rainy night, but we all came.
We read selections from our copybooks, listened to
music by the Mandolin Club and heard an address
by a minister from Bethlehem (Pennsylvania). He
spoke to us on the evils of the bicycle. There are six
members in my class, four girls and two boys. We all
hope to attend the upper school situated on Windy
Hill when we leave here. My father, however, does
not believe in higher education for females.

* * *

The teacher sees Paul Wilkes throwing snowballs in the
schoolyard. Later, when she questions him, he denies it.

"I watched you through the window," she states. "You
are telling me a lie, aren't you?"

Paul nods his head.

"Go to the bookshelf and bring me the life of Washington by Mr. Weems," the teacher orders.

Paul goes to the shelf and takes down *A History of the Life of General George Washington* by Mason Weems.

Mason Weems was born in 1760. He was a writer and preacher. His life of Washington was his most successful book. Written in 1800, it went through over fifty editions. Although many incidents in the book are ficticious, it was long a popular book. In 1876, it is found in many classrooms.

"Turn to the story of the cherry tree," the teacher tells Paul.

Paul finds the page.

"Now, read to me," she says.

"When George was about six years old, he was made the master of a hatchet, of which, like most boys, he was immoderately fond; and was constantly going about chopping everything that came in his way. One day, in the garden, where he often amused himself hacking his mother's pea-sticks, he unluckily tried the edge of his hatchet on the body of a beautiful young English cherry tree, which he marked so terribly, that I don't believe the tree ever got the better of it. The next morning the old gentleman, finding out what had befallen his tree, which, by the by, was a great favorite, came into the house; and with much warmth asked for the mischievous author, declaring at the same time that he would not have taken five guineas for his tree. Nobody could tell him anything about it. Presently George and his hatchet made their appearance. 'George,' said his father, 'do you know who killed that beautiful little cherry tree yonder in the garden?' This was a tough question; and George staggered under it for a moment; but quickly recovered himself: and looking at his father, with the sweet face of youth brightened with the inexpressible charm of all-conquering truth, he bravely called out, 'I can't tell a lie, Pa; you know I can't tell a lie. I did cut it with my hatchet."

"Remember that story, Paul," the teacher says.

"Yes, ma'am," Paul mumbles. "I'll try to be like General Washington and always tell the truth.

* * *

By 1876, doing "sums" has given way to arithmetic, the "art of doing computation." What is called "mental arithmetic" is popular. This is arithmetic done in the head and not on paper.

Arithmetic books in use cover addition, subtraction, multiplication, division, decimals, fractions and measurement.

Here are some problems from *The Common School Arithmetic:*

A house rents for $20 a year. Taxes amount to $15 a year. Repairs amount to $62 a year. What is the annual cost of the house?

($97.00)

At the General Store a man bought 5 yards of muslin at 12 cents a yard; a wooden bucket for 50 cents and three bags of barley at 6 cents a bag. How much does he owe the storekeeper?

($1.28)

If I sell a goat for $8, how many goats will bring me $96?

(12 goats)

If a farmer erects 72 feet of fencing each day, how much fencing will he complete in a fortnight?

(1008 feet)

If a man's salary is $7 per month and he saves 2 % of his salary each year, how much will he have saved in five years?

($8.40)

* * *

The following advice is written on the blackboard by the teacher at the Blue Creek District School:

Never tease dumb animals. Bees, wasps and hornets may become very cross by being teased, so as to sting innocent persons who are passing by their hives or nests.

Dogs, bulls and some other animals may be made very cross and dangerous by being wantonly teased and provoked.
Green apples and other unripe fruits are not wholesome.

Children who eat stone-fruit, such as apricots, cherries and plums, should not swallow the stones.
We should take care of our health. Many have become sick or lame by being careless.

* * *

Today is monthly report day at the Tilldale Common School, and nine-year-old Bill Barker is worried. His school work during the past month has been poor. He misspelled words, failed to solve arithmetic problems, and could not name the first five presidents. More than this, he was caught throwing spitballs at another boy.

The monthly report carries this message for parents:

It is hoped that the parents of the pupil, whose name appears above, will give this card not only a critical examination, but also demand its presentation at the end of each month. To verify this, a parent signature is requested.

A Cartoon of the Time
Shows the Student's View
of Examinations.

There is no way that he can avoid the consequence of his poor work and conduct. His father will probably spank him.

When the monthly reports are handed out, his fears are confirmed. He has a 4 in Arithmetic; a 5 in Spelling; a 3 in History and a 5 in Conduct. The card indicates that No. 1 signifies Very Good; No. 2—Good; No. 3—Middling; No. 4—Poor; No. 5—Very Poor.

Student reports are as old as schools, and by 1876, the report card is quite common. Many states require teachers to give parents a periodic report on student progress. Not only grades are reported, but also conduct and attendance.

Bill wishes that report cards had never been invented!

* * *

Dear Diary,
The first week of school is almost over. Only one
more day before the Sabbath holiday. I cannot wait.
Already I find school dreary, and long for summer
days.

We begin our lessons at eight o'clock in the
morning with a reading from Scripture recited by one
of the older girls. This is followed by a reading lesson
and then a grammar lesson.

At ten o'clock, we have a recess. We go to Miss
Water's room where we take tea and cakes.

After recess we begin our sewing and stitching
lessons. I am learning embroidery and the elements of
dressmaking. Lunch is at noon followed by an
afternoon of Arithmetic, Penmanship and Bible
Study. School is adjourned at five in the afternoon.

School Life in 1876

BREAKING THE RULES.

TONY LONGO TELLS ABOUT SCHOOL.

SCHOOLROOM PRANKS.

A GAME OF TOWN-BALL.

In the hallway of P.S. 24, these rules are posted for the scholars:

1. That any students who are late arriving at school shall be kept in during recess.

2. That whispering is prohibited at all times during school hours. Permission to whisper may be granted only if it concerns school matters.

3. That anyone leaving the seat without permission shall remain after school for 25 minutes.

4. That anyone throwing waste paper on the floor or causing any other untidiness shall be made to sweep the floor after school.

5. That anyone uttering profane words or found

fighting shall be locked in the closet for one
hour.

Despite the rules, James Porter and Samuel Smith are
found fighting in the classroom. James was cleaning slates
with a sponge. He dipped the sponge in a bucket of water
and squeezed it over Samuel Smith's head. Samuel uttered
a profane word and attempted to hit James with his geography book. At that moment, the teacher entered the room
and caught them. After some investigation, she stuck
James' head into the bucket. "This may cool off your de-
sire for pranks," she said. Then, she led both boys to the
schoolroom closet. She ordered them in and locked the
door behind them. They will stay there for one hour.

* * *

Tony Longo, the son of an Italian immigrant, tells about going to school in Chicago in 1876:

> I liked school. It was a big building only three blocks from where we lived. The teacher told us stories about General Grant and Abraham Lincoln and other great Americans. She also taught us how to read and write in English.
>
> When I first came to America from Italy, I did not even know the alphabet. The only letter I recognized was the letter B. My parents brought me to school because they wanted me to become an American. In a short while, I was able to write my name and recite the alphabet. Eventually, I was able to speak and write in English. At home, my parents spoke Italian. But, when my father spoke to me, he insisted that I answer in English.
>
> Sometimes the other pupils made fun of me. They mocked the Italian accent. "Hey, Tony!" they would call out. "You must be an Eye-talian! You eata da spaghetti!" Usually I pretended not to hear them. But one day I punched a boy in the nose and made him bleed. He called me an insulting name. When my father found out about it, he took his razor strap and whaled me. "You go to school to learn, not to fight!" he shouted.
>
> For the Centennial celebration, we had a pageant at school. I wore a white wig and played the role of

George Washington. My father was very proud. From that time on, he called me his "little Georgio Washington."

* * *

In a magazine article, Erwin House recalls his schooldays in 1876:

To a nervous child the discipline was, indeed, terrible. The long birch switches hanging on hooks against the wall haunted me day and night, from the time I entered school. And whenever there came an outburst between master and pupils, the thoughtless child often got the beating that should have fallen upon the mischief-maker. As the master was always quick to fly into a passion, the fun-loving boys were always happy to stir him up. It was an exciting sport, like bull-baiting, or like poking sticks through a fence at a cross dog. Sometimes the ferocious master showed an ability on his own part to get some fun out of the conflict, as when on one occasion in a school in Indiana, the boys were forbidden to attend a circus. Five or six of them went, in spite of the prohibition. The next morning the schoolmaster called them before him and said:

"So you went to the circus, did you?"

"Yes, sir."

"Well, the others did not get a chance to see the circus. I want you boys to show them what it looked like, and how the horses galloped around the ring.

You will join your hands in a circle about the stove.
Now start!"

With that he began whipping them as they trotted
around and around the stove.

It was great sport for the more daring boys to plant a handful of wild nuts in the ashes of the stove before the master arrived at the schoolhouse. It is the nature of these nuts to lie quietly in the hot ashes for about an hour and then explode, scattering hot coals all about. Nothing could be funnier than the wrath of the teacher as he went poking in the coals to find the remaining nuts, which generally eluded his search and popped away like torpedoes under his nose.

* * *

A newspaper reporter remembers a day in 1876:

We were playing "town-ball" in a field some distance from the schoolhouse. "Town-ball" is an old game from which the game of baseball evolved. Eastern boys called it "field-base." Western boys called it "town-ball." We used soft balls, primitive bats and no nonsense. There were no scores, but a catch or a cross-out put the whole side out, leaving the others to take the bat or "paddle," as we called it.

Either because the wind was blowing or because of our shouting, we failed to hear the ringing of the one o'clock bell. The afternoon wore on until someone suddenly realized we should be in the schoolroom. We dropped the game and ran, pell-mell, for the school. Arriving, we saw the girls all sitting in their places; the teacher was sitting silent. We shuffled into our seats and awaited the storm.

"The boys think that town-ball is more important than history and geography," she announced. "As a result, there will be no recess for the boys for the next five days."

The next day we composed a letter and placed it on the teacher's desk. We all signed our names. It read:

> *In regard to our offense of yesterday,*
> *we beg you to believe that it was not*
> *intentional. Considering this, could*
> *you not temper our punishment.*

The teacher gave each one of us a note in answer to our pleas. When opened, it simply read "NO!"

The Discipline of 1876

THE NEW TEACHER.

AN ITEM FROM WILL KNOX'S DIARY.

GOOD SOLDIERS.

AMONG THE POOR.

REFORM SCHOOLS AND ORPHANAGES.

"I ain't afraid of her," Tommy says.

"She's just a weak old lady," Billy adds.

"She's no bigger than a post rail," says Bart. "Why, she ain't got the muscle to harm anyone!"

The boys laugh together.

"What are you boys carrying on about?" a stern voice demands. It is Miss Parsons, the new teacher. "Get to your seats and behave yourselves," she shouts, rapping them on their heads with a stick. "I won't tolerate any nonsense. And if I catch you at any, I'll whale the daylight out of you!"

The boys rush to their desks and sit down. Tommy's eyes are as wide as saucers. Billy sits perfectly still, and Bart cringes.

"Thought you boys weren't afraid of her," a girl taunts.

The teachers of 1876, regardless of size or gender, are strict disciplinarians. They expect obedience and scholarship. And they resort to force when necessary.

A school committeeman advised a Rhode Island teacher, "There are times when muscle is more important than brain!"

* * *

Friday 14, 1876

At recess, Benjamin Wilson and I were running about the schoolroom trying to kick each other. Mr. Wilson appeared and allowed his stick to speak to us. We each received ten lashes with a birch bough. We were told that if it happens again, we will be locked in the schoolroom closet. In addition, Mr. Wilson did not speak to us for the entire day and gave us extra homework.

* * *

Ten-year-old Betty Cummins glances through a copy of her mother's book, *The Management of the Young.* Her mother left it on the parlor table. On one page she reads:

Let children revel in an absolute sense of freedom. Don't nag, be polite and use the word "don't" as little as possible.

Betty closes the book and hopes that her mother will take such good advice.

In 1876, the treatment of children is more enlightened,

especially among middle and upper class parents. Gone are the days of puritan discipline. Yet, Betty should read on. Later in the book the author states:

Like good soldiers, children must obey orders.

* * *

Life is harsh for many poor children. Petty cruelty and neglect are common in the factories and mines where children work. They toil from early morning until late at night without a break. In one factory in New York City, children are forced to work until midnight. Their boss throws cold water on them to keep them awake. In mines, breaker boys are prodded with sticks when they grow tired. Children carry scars from beatings and abuse.

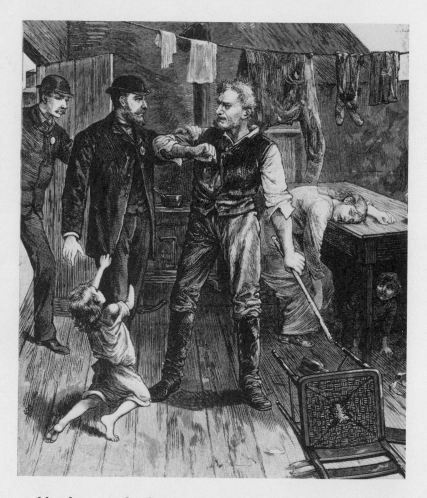

*Members of the Society for the Prevention of Cruelty
to Children Protect an Abused Child*

Conditions among working children are so terrible that a group is organized in New York. It is called the Society for the Prevention of Cruelty to Children.

* * *

"You better behave or I'll send you to reform school!"

This is a threat often made in 1876.

When parents cannot handle their children or when children commit crimes like stealing or damaging property, they are sent to reform school. Called industrial schools, they teach children "to be good." Here children work for seven hours each day and go to school for four hours. Often parents must pay for reform school. One such institution charges three dollars a day and a child must stay at least nine months. It promises to "turn a lazy boy into an industrious one." There are also reform schools for "viciously inclined young girls."

To be an orphan in 1876 is not much better. Orphans include children whose parents are sick, in the poorhouse, in prison or divorced. If neither parent can care for them, they enter an orphanage. The orphanage feeds and clothes them until they can work. Many orphans are sent into homes as domestic servants.

After School in 1876

Overnight, while the children in Millville slept, someone had posted great red, yellow and black signs on every tree trunk and fence in town.

CIRCUS
CLOWNS! WILD ANIMALS!
HIGH WIRE ARTISTS!

Introducing the most
difficult and dangerous
feats ever devised by
human ingenuity.

RIDERS FROM THE WILD WEST!
THE WORLD'S BIGGEST FAT LADY!

"The circus is coming!" children cry to each other. It is enough to turn heads from tending the cows or helping mother in the kitchen.

Finally, circus day arrives. The rumble of the gold and red circus wagons awakens the town. Before long, huge tents are erected in the lot behind Town Hall. Refreshment wagons and ticket wagons are wheeled into place. The smells of animals, hay and sawdust mingle with the aroma of hot popcorn. Men with great clusters of bright balloons walk through town. Millville will be able to see the tumbling Arabs, the fat lady, the snakecharmer and the wild west show. There will be tigers and lions and elephants. And, best of all, there will be no school today! Everyone is going to the circus.

The arrival of the circus is the most important event of the year. Like the Fourth of July and Christmas, it is eagerly awaited. Children dream about that summer day when the circus rolls into town. In small town America, the circus brings entertainment, excitement and wonder to an otherwise quiet existence.

* * *

Eleven-year-old Roy Hunter enjoys reading. His parents and his aunts and uncles give him books at Christmas and on birthdays. Roy has a set of the Rollo travel books. Written by Jacob Abbot, they tell about Rollo and his travels through many countries. He also owns a copy of *The Last of the Mohicans* by James Fenimore Cooper and a copy of Mary Mapes Dodge's, *Hans Brinker or The Silver Skates*. And last Christmas his Uncle Harry gave him a subscription to *St. Nicholas Magazine*. This is an outstanding magazine for children.

Roy also has a collection of dime novels. But he keeps them hidden in a box in the back of his closet. His mother calls the little paperback pamphlets "fantastical trash." Regardless, Roy enjoys the stories about pirates, hunters, soldiers and Indians. He and his friends often trade the "dimes" among themselves. At last count, Roy has twenty "dimes" hidden away in his closet.

* * *

In 1876, a national league of eight big-city professional baseball teams formed to set schedules and fix rules. Baseball originated out of several bat and ball games. It took on its first recognizable form around 1840. As the years went by, men's colleges took up the game. Then, in 1869, the first professional baseball team, the Cincinnati Red Stockings, toured the country taking on local teams. In this Centennial year, baseball is played by young and old alike on village fields and city streets.

"Baseball," writes Mark Twain, "is the very symbol . . . of the drive and push and rush and struggle of the raging, tearing and booming nineteenth century."

Football is another sport, although not as popular as baseball. It grew out of soccer and English rugby. In 1876 many people call the game "American rugby." Four colleges in the country—Rutgers, Columbia, Princeton and Yale—have set down rules for the game and play each other in competition.

In gardens and fields everywhere, Americans are playing croquet. It is so popular that wickets come equipped with candle holders for playing the game at night.

A new game imported from Bermuda is considered a proper sport for young ladies. It is called lawn tennis. Many young men have also taken up the game.

* * *

A group of boys in Centerville are on their way to Howell's Mill. It is a sunny, hot afternoon in late August, and the millpond water will be cool and refreshing.

The "Ole Swimmin' Hole" is as American as apple pie. Over one hundred years before Benjamin Franklin remembered his "swimmin' hole" in Boston.

Arriving at the millpond, the boys take off their clothing and swim and dive as naked as jaybirds. Swimming attire may be required for ocean bathing, but nothing is required at the "Ole Swimmin' Hole."

There are other boys in Centerville who prefer the river. A high bank of slippery clay makes a fine slide into the water. You can also swim out to Baker's Island in the middle of the river. But at the millpond you can climb onto a high stone wall and dive into the water. It also offers

more privacy. Last month, a group of boys were surprised by some ladies out for a riverbank stroll. Though the ladies looked the other way, the boys stayed under water until they passed.

In every city and small town across America, there are swimming holes. River, lake, pond or stream, they offer fun on hot summer days.

* * *

In American cities children play in streets, parks and vacant lots.

Skating in Central Park

Sadly, for many poor children there is little time to play. One Chicago resident records:

The streets are full of ragged urchins whose childhood has been stolen away.

For more fortunate children, the city is an exciting place. The activity of city life is entertainment enough. There are passing carriages and trolley cars and busy sidewalks. Then, there are the parks. New York has Central Park; Boston has its Commons and Philadelphia has Fairmont Park. Most cities have established parks for their residents. Here children can romp and play or explore tiny forests. They can watch birds or chase squirrels. They can sail toy boats in small lakes and climb footpaths over little hills.

The streets of the cities are alive with children. Boys play tag while girls play hopscotch. In the wintertime snowmen line the sidewalks and sleds glide over the snow-covered streets. Life and activity is all around. There is rarely a moment of boredom.

* * *

Dearest Cousin Anna,
Here I am at the Centennial Exhibition in Philadelphia—249 buildings on 285 acres of Fairmont Park for fifty cents admission.
I have seen fire engines, railroad cars, totem poles, machinery, stuffed birds, Japanese screens and more

*paintings and sculpture than I knew existed. I have
eaten an abundance of popcorn and swallowed gallons
of root beer.*

*The crowds are immense. There are folks here
from all over the country. Yesterday, I spoke with a
girl from California. She and her family crossed the
nation by railroad. Just imagine!*

*To my mind, the most exciting sight at the
Exhibition is the arm and torch of the unfinished
Statue of Liberty. It stands forty feet high. Think
what the statue will be when it is completed and
standing in New York harbor!*

*I do wish you could have come along. We can only
see one Centennial celebration in a lifetime and this
is a wonderful experience.*

*As ever,
Helen*

Our Historical Journey Ends

Now we leave behind the schools and children of 1876.
Since that time America has marked another milestone.
We are moving into a third century. Much has happened.
Our society has changed; our way of life has changed and
going to school has changed.

The Old-Fashioned Schoolhouse

The America of 1876 belongs to history. The children,
the teachers and the schools are but a memory. Yet they
are a part of today and will be a part of tomorrow. The
past is always with us. It is the foundation on which we
build.

Bibliography

1. Boorstin and others. *We Americans*. National Geographic Society, Washington, D.C. 1975.

2. Butts, R. Freeman. *A Cultural History of Education*. McGraw Hill. 1947.

3. Cubberly, Elwood P. *Public Education in the United States*. Houghton Mifflin. 1934.

4. Eggleston, Edward. *The Hoosier Schoolmaster*. Grosset & Dunlap. 1913.

5. Elsbree, Willard. *The American Teacher*. American Book. 1939.

6. French, William. *America's Educational Tradition*. D.C. Heath. 1964.

7. Garland, Hamlin. *Son of the Middle Border*. Macmillan. 1923.

8. Miller, George. *The Academy System in the State of New York*. 1922.

9. Swartzlander, Ellen (transcribed by). *Mister Andrew's School*. Bucks County Historical Society. 1958.

10. Wickersham, J.P. *A History of Education in Pennsylvania*. Inquirer Publishing. 1886.